I0652581

To:
_____

From:
_____

Message:
_____

_____

_____

_____

101 *Seeds of* FAITH

CHRISTIAN ART PUBLISHERS

Published by Christian Art Publishers
PO Box 1599, Vereeniging, 1930, RSA

© 2015
First edition 2015

Cover designed by Christian Art Publishers

Images used under license from Shutterstock.com

Printed in China

ISBN 978-1-4321-1403-9

17 18 19 20 21 22 23 24 25 26 – 11 10 9 8 7 6 5 4 3 2

"Truly I tell you, if you have faith as small as a mustard seed, you can say to this mountain, 'Move from here to there,' and it will move. Nothing will be impossible for you."

Matthew 17:20

01

Faith is not knowing what the future holds, but knowing who holds the future.

Trust in the LORD with all your heart and lean not on your own understanding; in all your ways submit to Him, and He will make your paths straight.

Proverbs 3:5-6 NIV

02

You can have peace
in the midst of the
storm when you know
that God is in control.

You will keep in perfect peace those
whose minds are steadfast, because
they trust in You.
Isaiah 26:3 NIV

03 "It is not the strength of your faith that saves you, but the strength of Him upon whom you rely."

Charles H. Spurgeon

"The LORD your God is with you, the Mighty Warrior who saves. He will take great delight in you; in His love He will no longer rebuke you, but will rejoice over you with singing."

Zephaniah 3:17 NIV

04 "Feed your fears and your faith will starve. Feed your faith, and your fears will."

Max Lucado

Give your burdens to the LORD, and He will take care of you. He will not permit the godly to slip and fall.

Psalm 55:22 NLT

05

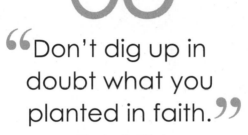

"Don't dig up in doubt what you planted in faith."

Elisabeth Elliot

When you ask, you must believe and not doubt, because the one who doubts is like a wave of the sea, blown and tossed by the wind.

James 1:6 NIV

06

Faith is not believing God can, but knowing that He will.

Without faith it is impossible to please God, because anyone who comes to Him must believe that He exists and that He rewards those who earnestly seek Him.

Hebrews 11:6 NIV

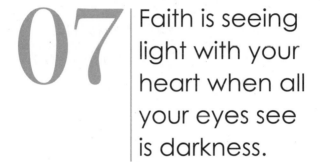

07 Faith is seeing light with your heart when all your eyes see is darkness.

Faith is the confidence that what we hope
for will actually happen; it gives us assurance
about things we cannot see.

Hebrews 11:1 NLT

08 | Worry ends where faith in God begins.

Don't worry about anything; instead, pray about everything. Tell God what you need, and thank Him for all He has done. Then you will experience God's peace, which exceeds anything we can understand. His peace will guard your hearts and minds as you live in Christ Jesus.

Philippians 4:6-7 NLT

09

"Faith is like a bird that feels dawn breaking and sings while it is still dark."

Scandinavian Proverb

Let the morning bring me word of Your unfailing love, for I have put my trust in You. Show me the way I should go, for to You I entrust my life.

Psalm 143:8 NIV

10

"" My hope is built on nothing less
than Jesus' blood and righteousness.
I dare not trust the sweetest frame,
but wholly lean on Jesus' name.
On Christ, the solid Rock, I stand;
all other ground is sinking sand. ""

Edward Mote

Jesus answered, "I am the way and the
truth and the life. No one comes to the
Father except through Me."

John 14:6 NIV

11

"Faith sees the invisible, believes the unbelievable, and receives the impossible."

Corrie ten Boom

For we live by faith, not by sight.
2 Corinthians 5:7 NIV

12 | With Christ we can weather any storm.

He calmed the storm to a whisper
and stilled the waves.

Psalm 107:29 NLT

13

"If we desire our faith to be strengthened, we should not shrink from opportunities where our faith may be tried, and therefore, through trial, be strengthened."

George Müller

For you know that when your faith is tested, your endurance has a chance to grow.

James 1:3 NLT

14

> ❝Faith expects from God what is beyond all expectation.❞
>
> Andrew Murray

By faith Noah, when warned about things not yet seen, in holy fear built an ark to save his family. By his faith he condemned the world and became heir of the righteousness that is in keeping with faith.

Hebrews 11:7 NIV

15

"Faith makes all things possible. Love makes all things easy."

D. L. Moody

The only thing that counts is faith expressing itself through love.

Galatians 5:6 NIV

16 | "Storms make oaks take deeper roots."

George Herbert

Let your roots grow down into Him,
and let your lives be built on Him.
Then your faith will grow strong in the
truth you were taught, and you will
overflow with thankfulness.

Colossians 2:7 NLT

17

God has placed you where you are right now for a reason; trust Him to work everything out.

"For I know the plans I have for you," declares the LORD, "plans to prosper you and not to harm you, plans to give you hope and a future."

Jeremiah 29:11 NIV

18

Prayer is the road to heaven, but faith opens the door.

"You can pray for anything, and if you have faith, you will receive it."
Matthew 21:22 NLT

19

"In faith there is enough light for those who want to believe and enough shadows to blind those who don't."

Blaise Pascal

Jesus spoke to the people once more and said, "I am the light of the world. If you follow Me, you won't have to walk in darkness, because you will have the light that leads to life."

John 8:12 NLT

"God loves
with a great
love the man
whose heart is
bursting with a
passion for the
impossible."

William Booth

Then Jesus told them, "I tell you the truth, if
you have faith and don't doubt, you can do
things like this and much more. You can even
say to this mountain, 'May you be lifted up
and thrown into the sea,' and it will happen."

Matthew 21:21 NLT

21

"You find no difficulty in trusting the Lord with the management of the universe and all the outward creation, and can your case be any more complex or difficult than these, that you need to be anxious or troubled about His management of it?"

Hannah Whitall Smith

I will say of the LORD, "He is my refuge and my fortress, my God, in whom I trust."
Psalm 91:2 NIV

22

"By faith we are taken into Christ, made at once safe from holy wrath against sin, and kept safe from all perils and penalties. He, our divine Redeemer, becomes to us the new sphere of harmony and unity with God and His law, with His life and His holiness."

A. T. Pierson

For it is by grace you have been saved, through faith – and this is not from yourselves, it is the gift of God – not by works, so that no one can boast.

Ephesians 2:8-9 NIV

23

"The Bible recognizes no faith that does not lead to obedience, nor does it recognize any obedience that does not spring from faith. The two are at opposite sides of the same coin."

A. W. Tozer

But these are written that you may believe that Jesus is the Messiah, the Son of God, and that by believing you may have life in His name.

John 20:31 NIV

24 Faith in God involves faith in His timing.

And we know that in all things God works for the good of those who love Him, who have been called according to His purpose.

Romans 8:28 NIV

25

"Faith is to believe what we do not see, and the reward of this faith is to see what we believe."

St. Augustine

Now we see things imperfectly, like puzzling reflections in a mirror, but then we will see everything with perfect clarity. All that I know now is partial and incomplete, but then I will know everything completely, just as God now knows me completely.

1 Corinthians 13:12 NLT

26

"God always gives
His best to those
who leave the
choice with Him."

Jim Elliot

Commit everything you do to the LORD.
Trust Him, and He will help you.

Psalm 37:5 NLT

27

"Be assured,
if you walk
with Him and
look to Him,
and expect
help from Him,
He will never
fail you."

George Müller

Keep your lives free from the love of money
and be content with what you have, because
God has said, "Never will I leave you;
never will I forsake you."

Hebrews 13:5 NIV

28

"If faith produces no works, I see that faith is not a living tree. Thus faith and works together grow; no separate life they ever can know. They're soul and body, hand and heart; what God hath joined, let no man part."

Hannah More

Just as the body is dead without breath, so also faith is dead without good works.

James 2:26 NLT

29

"Faith is the root of all blessings. Believe, and you shall be saved; believe, and your needs must be satisfied; believe, and you cannot but be comforted."

Jeremy Taylor

Trust in the LORD and do good. Then you will live safely in the land and prosper.
Psalm 37:3 NLT

30

"The beginning of anxiety is the end of faith, and the beginning of true faith is the end of anxiety."

George Müller

Be still before the LORD and wait patiently for Him; do not fret when people succeed in their ways, when they carry out their wicked schemes.

Psalm 37:7 NIV

31

"A simple, childlike faith in a Divine Friend solves all the problems that come to us by land or sea."

Helen Keller

"Let the little children come to Me, and do not hinder them, for the kingdom of God belongs to such as these. Truly I tell you, anyone who will not receive the kingdom of God like a little child will never enter it."

Mark 10:14-15 NIV

 **32** | "The steps of faith fall on the seeming void, and find the rock beneath."

John Greenleaf Whittier

"The LORD is my rock, my fortress, and my Savior; my God is my rock, in whom I find protection. He is my shield, the power that saves me, and my place of safety."

2 Samuel 22:2-3 NLT

33

> ❝The safest place in all the world is in the will of God, and the safest protection in all the world is the name of God.❞
>
> Warren Wiersbe

The name of the LORD is a strong fortress; the godly run to Him and are safe.

Proverbs 18:10 NLT

34

Fear can keep us up all night long, but faith makes one fine pillow.

In peace I will lie down and sleep, for You alone, O LORD, will keep me safe.

Psalm 4:8 NLT

35

"Our praying, to be strong, must be buttressed by holy living. The life of faith perfects the prayer of faith."

E. M. Bounds

The prayer of a righteous person is powerful and effective.

James 5:16 NIV

36

"To love means loving the unlovable. To forgive means pardoning the unpardonable. Faith means believing the unbelievable. Hope means hoping when everything seems hopeless."

G. K. Chesterton

Why, my soul, are you downcast?
Why so disturbed within me?
Put your hope in God, for I will yet
praise Him, my Savior and my God.

Psalm 43:5 NIV

37

"Faith makes: The uplook good, the outlook bright, the inlook favorable and the future glorious."

V. Raymond Edman

For in this hope we were saved. But hope that is seen is no hope at all. Who hopes for what they already have? But if we hope for what we do not yet have, we wait for it patiently.

Romans 8:24-25 NIV

38

" Faith is deliberate
confidence in the
character of God
whose ways you
may not understand
at the time. "

Oswald Chambers

God is not a man, so He does not lie. He
is not human, so He does not change His
mind. Has He ever spoken and failed to
act? Has He ever promised and not
carried it through?

Numbers 23:19 NLT

39 | "I know whom I have believed. (Latin – Scio cui credidi)"

Blaise Pascal

For this reason I also suffer these things;
nevertheless I am not ashamed, for I
know whom I have believed and am
persuaded that He is able to keep what
I have committed to Him until that Day.

2 Timothy 1:12 NKJV

40

"It is impossible for that man to despair who remembers that his Helper is omnipotent."

Jeremy Taylor

"I am the LORD, the God of all mankind. Is anything too hard for Me?"

Jeremiah 32:27 NIV

41

" Many Christians estimate difficulty in the light of their own resources, and thus they attempt very little and they always fail. All giants have been weak men who did great things for God because they reckoned on His power and presence to be with them. "

Hudson Taylor

Each time He said, "My grace is all you need. My power works best in weakness." So now I am glad to boast about my weaknesses, so that the power of Christ can work through me. That's why I take pleasure in my weaknesses. For when I am weak, then I am strong.

2 Corinthians 12:9-10 NLT

42

"Faith isn't the ability to believe long and far into the misty future. It's simply taking God at His Word and taking the next step."

Joni Eareckson Tada

The steps of a good man are ordered by the LORD, and He delights in his way. Though he fall, he shall not be utterly cast down; for the LORD upholds him with His hand.

Psalm 37:23-24 NKJV

43

"He who created us without our help will not save us without our consent."

St. Augustine

Seek the LORD while He may be found; call on Him while He is near. Let the wicked forsake their ways and the unrighteous their thoughts. Let them turn to the LORD, and He will have mercy on them, and to our God, for He will freely pardon.

Isaiah 55:6-7 NIV

44

"What now is faith? Nothing other than the certainty that what God says is true."

Andrew Murray

"When the Spirit of truth comes, He will guide you into all truth. He will not speak on His own but will tell you what He has heard. He will tell you about the future."

John 16:13 NLT

45

"**Every tomorrow has two handles. We can take hold of it with the handle of anxiety or the handle of faith.**"

Henry Ward Beecher

"Can all your worries add a single moment to your life? And if worry can't accomplish a little thing like that, what's the use of worrying over bigger things?"

Luke 12:25-26 NLT

46

If God brings you to it, He will bring you through it.

Even when I walk through the darkest valley, I will not be afraid, for You are close beside me. Your rod and Your staff protect and comfort me.

Psalm 23:4 NLT

47

"When a train goes through a tunnel and it gets dark, you don't throw away the ticket and jump off. You sit still and trust the engineer."

Corrie ten Boom

Whoever dwells in the shelter of the Most High will rest in the shadow of the Almighty.

Psalm 91:1 NIV

48 | "He who
sends the
storm steers
the vessel."

Thomas Adams

The one who calls you is faithful,
and He will do it.

1 Thessalonians 5:24 NIV

"If we cannot believe God when circumstances seem to be against us, we do not believe Him at all."

Charles H. Spurgeon

But blessed is the one who trusts in the LORD, whose confidence is in Him. They will be like a tree planted by the water that sends out its roots by the stream. It does not fear when heat comes; its leaves are always green. It has no worries in a year of drought and never fails to bear fruit.

Jeremiah 17:7-8 NIV

50

"Faith is to the soul what life is to the body. Prayer is to faith what breath is to the body. How a person can live and not breathe is past my comprehension, and how a person can believe and not pray is past my comprehension too. "

J. C. Ryle

"You can ask for anything in My name, and I will do it, so that the Son can bring glory to the Father. Yes, ask Me for anything in My name, and I will do it!"

John 14:13-14 NLT

"If you wish to know God, you must know His Word. If you wish to perceive His power, you must see how He works by His Word. If you wish to know His purpose before it comes to pass, you can only discover it by His Word."

Charles H. Spurgeon

51

God's way is perfect. All the LORD's promises prove true. He is a shield for all who look to Him for protection.

Psalm 18:30 NLT

52

"Never be afraid to trust an unknown future to a known God."

Corrie ten Boom

Whom have I in heaven but You? And earth has nothing I desire besides You. My flesh and my heart may fail, but God is the strength of my heart and my portion forever.

Psalm 73:25-26 NIV

53

> **❝**Faith is a reasoning trust, a trust which reckons thoughtfully and confidently upon the trustworthiness of God.**❞**

John Stott

By faith we understand that the entire universe was formed at God's command, that what we now see did not come from anything that can be seen.

Hebrews 11:3 NLT

54

" Faith consists, not
in ignorance, but
in knowledge, and
that, not only of God,
but also of the
divine will. "

John Calvin

Then Job replied to the LORD: "I know
that You can do all things; no purpose
of Yours can be thwarted."

Job 42:1-2 NIV

55 | "Faith is taking the first step even when you don't see the whole staircase."

Martin Luther King, Jr.

He will not let your foot slip – He who watches over you will not slumber.

Psalm 121:3 NIV

56 | "Trust God to weave your little thread into the great web, though the pattern shows it not yet."

George MacDonald

How abundant are the good things that You have stored up for those who fear You, that You bestow in the sight of all, on those who take refuge in You.

Psalm 31:19 NIV

57

"There's a pardon for every sinner on the topside of the earth, but you have to call for it by faith before it becomes yours. In other words, you have to trust Christ as your Savior."

J. Vernon McGee

For God so loved the world that He gave His one and only Son, that whoever believes in Him shall not perish but have eternal life.

John 3:16 NIV

58

"As we trust God to give us wisdom for today's decisions, He will lead us a step at a time into what He wants us to be doing in the future."

Theodore Epp

The wisdom that is from above is first pure, then peaceable, gentle, willing to yield, full of mercy and good fruits, without partiality and without hypocrisy.

James 3:17 NKJV

59

"Nothing is too great and nothing is too small to commit into the hands of the Lord."

A. W. Pink

"Don't be afraid, for I am with you. Don't be discouraged, for I am your God. I will strengthen you and help you. I will hold you up with My victorious right hand."

Isaiah 41:10 NLT

60

"I believe in Christianity as I believe that the sun has risen: not only because I see it, but because by it I see every-thing else."

C. S. Lewis

For ever since the world was created, people have seen the earth and sky. Through everything God made, they can clearly see His invisible qualities – His eternal power and divine nature. So they have no excuse for not knowing God.

Romans 1:20 NLT

61

"If our love were but more simple, we should take Him at His word; and our lives would be all sunshine in the sweetness of the Lord."

Frederick W. Faber

Love the LORD your God with all your heart and with all your soul and with all your strength.

Deuteronomy 6:5 NIV

62

"It is not worrying, but rather trusting and abiding in the peace of God that will crush anything that Satan tries to do to us. If the Lord created the world out of chaos, He can easily deal with any problem that we have."

Rick Joyner

I know the LORD is always with me. I will not be shaken, for He is right beside me.
Psalm 16:8 NLT

63

"Trust the past to God's mercy, the present to God's love, and the future to God's providence."

St. Augustine

Can you search out the deep things of God? Can you find out the limits of the Almighty? They are higher than heaven – what can you do? Deeper than Sheol – what can you know? Their measure is longer than the earth and broader than the sea.

Job 11:7-9 NKJV

64

"We cannot always trace God's hand, but we can always trust God's heart."

Charles H. Spurgeon

The eyes of all look expectantly to You, and You give them their food in due season. You open Your hand and satisfy the desire of every living thing.

Psalm 145:15-16 NKJV

65

"God's commands are designed to guide you to life's very best. You will not obey Him, if you do not believe Him and trust Him. You cannot believe Him if you do not love Him. You cannot love Him unless you know Him."

Henry Blackaby

Jesus replied, "Anyone who loves Me will obey My teaching. My Father will love them, and We will come to them and make Our home with them."

John 14:23 NIV

66

"Either we are adrift in chaos or we are individuals, created, loved, upheld and placed purposefully, exactly where we are. Can you believe that? Can you trust God for that?"

Elisabeth Elliot

The LORD has established His throne in heaven, and His kingdom rules over all.

Psalm 103:19 NKJV

67

"Let God enlarge you when you are going through distress. He can do it. You can't do it, and others can't do it for you."

Warren Wiersbe

It is better to trust in the LORD than to put confidence in man. It is better to trust in the LORD than to put confidence in princes.

Psalm 118:8-9 NKJV

68

"Faith takes God without any ifs."

D. L. Moody

But he [Thomas] said to them, "Unless I see the nail marks in His hands and put my finger where the nails were, and put my hand into His side, I will not believe." Then He [Jesus] said to Thomas, "Put your finger here; see My hands. Reach out your hand and put it into My side. Stop doubting and believe." Thomas said to Him, "My Lord and my God!" Then Jesus told him, "Because you have seen Me, you have believed; blessed are those who have not seen and yet have believed."

John 20:25, 27-29 NIV

69

"Thou canst not tell how rich a dowry sorrow gives the soul, how firm a faith and eagle sight of God."

Henry Alford

He gives power to the weak and strength to the powerless. Even youths will become weak and tired, and young men will fall in exhaustion. But those who trust in the LORD will find new strength. They will soar high on wings like eagles. They will run and not grow weary. They will walk and not faint.

Isaiah 40:29-31 NLT

70

"Real satisfaction comes not in understanding God's motives, but in understanding His character, in trusting in His promises, and in leaning on Him and resting in Him as the Sovereign who knows what He is doing and does all things well."

Joni Eareckson Tada

"Only I can tell you the future before it even happens. Everything I plan will come to pass, for I do whatever I wish."

Isaiah 46:10 NLT

71

"Standing on the promises that cannot fail, when the howling storms of doubt and fear assail, by the living Word of God I shall prevail, standing on the promises of God."

Russell K. Carter

Let us hold unswervingly to the hope we profess, for He who promised is faithful.

Hebrews 10:23 NIV

72

"The will of God for your life is simply that you submit yourself to Him each day and say, 'Father, Your will for today is mine. Your pleasure for today is mine. Your work for today is mine. I trust You to be God. You lead me today and I will follow.'"

Kay Arthur

So humble yourselves under the mighty power of God, and at the right time He will lift you up in honor.

1 Peter 5:6 NLT

73

“Faith never knows where it is being led, but it loves and knows the One who is leading.”

Oswald Chambers

And so we know and rely on the love God has for us. God is love. Whoever lives in love lives in God, and God in them.

1 John 4:16 NIV

74

"I'm so glad I learned to trust Thee, Precious Jesus, Savior, Friend; and I know that Thou art with me, wilt be with me to the end."

Louisa M. R. Stead

For I am convinced that neither death nor life, neither angels nor demons, neither the present nor the future, nor any powers, neither height nor depth, nor anything else in all creation, will be able to separate us from the love of God that is in Christ Jesus our Lord.

Romans 8:38-39 NIV

"If Jesus Christ be God and died for me, then no sacrifice can be too great for me to make for Him."

C. T. Studd

75

Then Jesus said to His disciples, "Whoever wants to be My disciple must deny themselves and take up their cross and follow Me."

Matthew 16:24 NIV

76

"Lord, whatever You want, wherever You want it, and whenever You want it, that's what I want."

Richard Baxter

I know what it is to be in need, and I know what it is to have plenty. I have learned the secret of being content in any and every situation, whether well fed or hungry, whether living in plenty or in want. I can do all this through Him who gives me strength.

Philippians 4:12-13 NIV

77

"It is not the cares of today, but the cares of tomorrow, that weigh a man down. For the needs of today we have corresponding strength given. For the morrow we are told to trust. It is not ours yet. It is when tomorrow's burden is added to the burden of today that the weight is more than a man can bear."

George MacDonald

"Therefore do not worry about tomorrow, for tomorrow will worry about its own things. Sufficient for the day is its own trouble."
Matthew 6:34 NKJV

78

> ❝Christians, who have given themselves into the care and keeping of the Lord Jesus, still continue to bend beneath the weight of their burden, and often go weary and heavy laden throughout the whole length of their journey.❞

Hannah Whitall Smith

Then Jesus said, "Come to Me, all of you who are weary and carry heavy burdens, and I will give you rest. Take My yoke upon you. Let Me teach you, because I am humble and gentle at heart, and you will find rest for your souls. For My yoke is easy to bear, and the burden I give you is light."

Matthew 11:28-30 NLT

79

"Knowing that God is faithful, it really helps me to not be captivated by worry."

Josh McDowell

The faithful love of the LORD never ends! His mercies never cease. Great is His faithfulness; His mercies begin afresh each morning.

Lamentations 3:22-23 NLT

80

"There is more safety with Christ in the tempest, than without Christ in the calmest waters."

Henry Martyn

He is the Rock, His works are perfect, and all His ways are just. A faithful God who does no wrong, upright and just is He.

Deuteronomy 32:4 NIV

81

"God's strength behind you, His concern for you, His love within you, and His arms beneath you are more than sufficient for the job ahead of you."

William A. Ward

He will cover you with His feathers. He will shelter you with His wings. His faithful promises are your armor and protection.

Psalm 91:4 NLT

82

"Trust is not a passive state of mind. It is a vigorous act of the soul by which we choose to lay hold on the promises of God and cling to them despite the adversity that at times seeks to overwhelm us."

Jerry Bridges

"This is My command – be strong and courageous! Do not be afraid or discouraged. For the LORD your God is with you wherever you go."

Joshua 1:9 NLT

83

"God never made a promise that was too good to be true."

D. L. Moody

The Lord is not slow in keeping His
promise, as some understand slowness.
Instead He is patient with you,
not wanting anyone to perish,
but everyone to come to repentance.

2 Peter 3:9 NIV

84

"God never calls His people to accomplish anything without promising to supply their every need."

Charles Swindoll

And my God shall supply all your
need according to His riches
in glory by Christ Jesus.

Philippians 4:19 NKJV

85

"Every promise of Scripture is a writing of God, which may be pleaded before Him with this reasonable request, "Do as Thou hast said." The Heavenly Father will not break His Word to His own child."

Charles H. Spurgeon

"Heaven and earth will pass away, but My words will by no means pass away."
Matthew 24:35 NKJV

86

In the happy moments, praise God. In the difficult moments, seek God. In the quiet moments, worship God. In the painful moments, trust God. In every moment, thank God.

Never stop praying. Be thankful in all circumstances, for this is God's will for you who belong to Christ Jesus.

1 Thessalonians 5:17-18 NLT

87

God has placed you where you're at in this very moment for a reason, remember that and trust that He is working everything out.

He has made everything beautiful in its time. He has also set eternity in the human heart; yet no one can fathom what God has done from beginning to end.

Ecclesiastes 3:11 NIV

88

We can't always see where the road leads, but God promises there is something better up ahead – we just have to trust Him.

When I am afraid, I put my trust in You.
In God, whose word I praise – in God
I trust and am not afraid.

Psalm 56:3-4 NIV

Thank God for what you have. Trust God for what you need.

"I will be your God throughout your lifetime – until your hair is white with age. I made you, and I will care for you, I will carry you along and save you."

Isaiah 46:4 NLT

90

"Oh, how great peace and quietness would he possess who should cut off all vain anxiety and place all his confidence in God."

Thomas à Kempis

"I have told you all this so that you may have peace in Me. Here on earth you will have many trials and sorrows. But take heart, because I have overcome the world."

John 16:33 NLT

91

"Today, God gives each of us a choice as we face life's challenges. We can deliberately choose to follow Him and rest in His truth and promises or we can choose to surrender our minds to pointless worry and the resulting stress that worry brings."

Katherine Walden

"Don't let your hearts be troubled. Trust in God, and trust also in Me."

John 14:1 NLT

92 | Faith is the bridge between where I am and where God is taking me.

Put your hope in the LORD. Travel steadily along His path.

Psalm 37:34 NLT

93

Have faith in Jesus.
Put your hope in His
name. Place your life
in His hands.

"And His name will be the
hope of all the world."
Matthew 12:21 NLT

94

"The presence of hope in the invincible sovereignty of God drives out fear. "

John Piper

Accept the way God does things, for who can straighten what He has made crooked? Enjoy prosperity while you can, but when hard times strike, realize that both come from God.

Ecclesiastes 7:13-14 NLT

95

"God is the only one who can make the valley of trouble a door of hope."

Catherine Marshall

And so, Lord, where do I put my hope?
My only hope is in You.

Psalm 39:7 NLT

96

God has perfect timing; never early, never late. In the end it's worth the wait.

I wait for the LORD, my soul waits, and in His word I do hope. My soul waits for the Lord more than those who watch for the morning – yes, more than those who watch for the morning.

Psalm 130:5-6 NKJV

97

"Faith is the victory!
Faith is the victory! O
glorious victory, that
overcomes the world."

John H. Yates

For every child of God defeats this
evil world, and we achieve this victory
through our faith.

1 John 5:4 NLT

98

> **"Be not dismayed**
> **whate'er betide,**
> **God will take care of you;**
> **beneath His wings of love abide,**
> **God will take care of you."**

Civilla D. Martin

Give all your worries and cares to God,
for He cares about you.

1 Peter 5:7 NLT

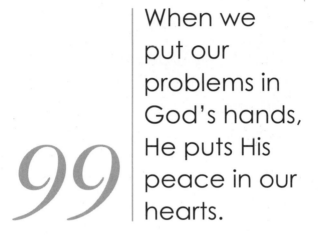

When we put our problems in God's hands, He puts His peace in our hearts.

"Though the mountains be shaken and the hills be removed, yet My unfailing love for you will not be shaken nor My covenant of peace be removed," says the LORD, who has compassion on you.

Isaiah 54:10 NIV

100

"When you get to the end
of all the light you know and
it's time to step into the darkness of the unknown, faith
is knowing that one of two
things shall happen: either
you will be given something
solid to stand on, or you will
be taught how to fly."

Edward Teller

My salvation and my honor depend on God;
He is my mighty rock, my refuge.

Psalm 62:7 NIV

101

"God is God. Because He is God, He is worthy of my trust and obedience. I will find rest nowhere but in His holy will, a will that is unspeakably beyond my largest notions of what He is up to. "

Elisabeth Elliot

Have you never heard? Have you never understood? The LORD is the everlasting God, the Creator of all the earth. He never grows weak or weary. No one can measure the depths of His understanding.

Isaiah 40:28 NLT